SKELETONS

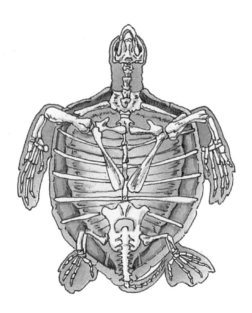

written by D Harper
illustrated by S Boni *and* L R Galante

Ladybird

CONTENTS

WHAT IS A SKELETON?

A skeleton is the framework of an animal. It supports the body and holds it in shape. It also protects parts of the body from injury and helps its owner to move. In some animals the skeleton is inside the body, in others it is on the outside, and some animals have no skeleton at all.

Internal skeletons

We have a skeleton inside our bodies. This kind of skeleton supports our bodies in the same way as steel girders support a skyscraper. An internal skeletal frame holds a body or building up, and supports its weight.

Framework of a skyscraper

A human skeleton

5

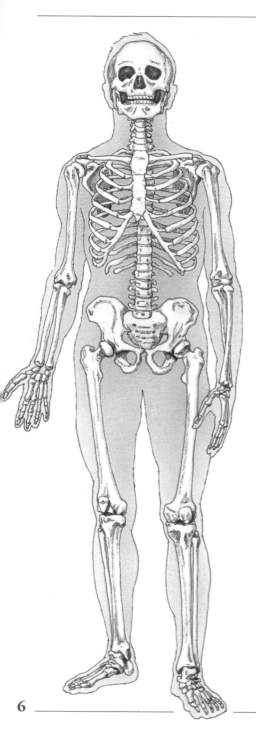

HUMAN SKELETONS

In some parts of your body, your bones are closer to the surface than others. If you press the sides of your wrists or ankles, you will be able to feel the hard bones under the skin. Other bones are buried too deep under big muscles to be felt easily.

Where bones touch each other, there is often an extra support, provided by **ligaments**. These act like tight tape, helping to bind your bones together and reinforce them. Your muscles are fixed to bones by **tendons**.

Staying upright
Your skeleton does the same job as the poles in a tent. It stops you from collapsing into a heap.

ANIMAL SKELETONS

Animals with backbones, or spines, are called **vertebrates.** They all have a skull, which protects the brain, at the top of the spine. Vertebrates have ribs at the sides of their bodies, and limbs, wings or fins supported by bones. All skeletons are adapted to an individual animal's lifestyle. For example, our skeleton is adapted for walking on two legs.

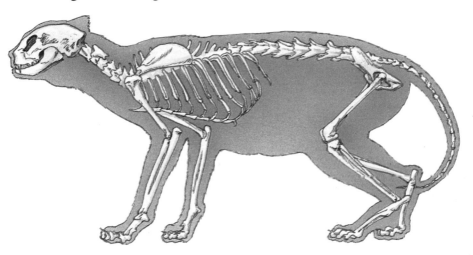

A cat's skeleton
Some animal skeletons, like a cat's, include a long tail. This helps the animal to jump and keep its balance.

A cat is a successful hunter and its skeleton is specially adapted for this activity – four long legs help a cat to run fast.

Fish bones
Fish use their bony fins, flat tail and muscular bodies for swimming.

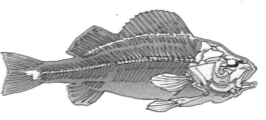

INSIDE BONES

Skeletons are made of bones that have to be light and strong. A bone has a thick, outer wall of compact bone and a softer part inside, called spongy bone.

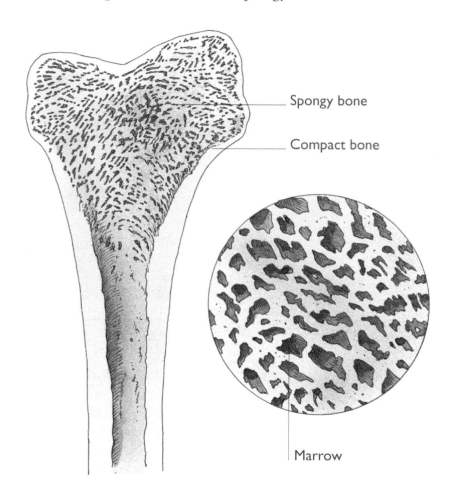

Spongy bone

Compact bone

Marrow

Healthy bones
Minerals, mainly calcium, vitamins and water help keep bones healthy and in tip-top condition.

Magnified spongy bone
The honeycomb-like holes are filled with **marrow**, which makes **red blood cells**.

BREAKING BONES

If you break a bone, it will slowly mend itself. It may need the help of a plaster cast to hold it straight while the fractured parts repair themselves. Doctors use X-rays to look at **fractures** and to check that bones are healing.

Seeing bones with X-rays

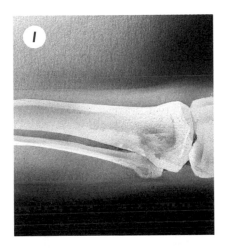

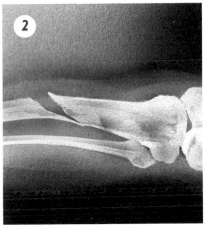

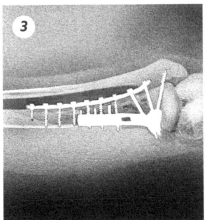

REVEALING BROKEN BONES

1 An X-ray of a normal, healthy bone.
2 An X-ray of a broken bone.
3 If a bone is badly broken, a surgeon may need to attach a metal plate to keep the fractured parts in place, as seen in this X-ray.

SHELLS AND EXOSKELETONS

Animals that do not have backbones are called **invertebrates**. Many animals, such as crabs or insects, have hard, outer casings called **exoskeletons**. Other animals, such as mussels or snails, are protected by shells, which are also exoskeletons. Exoskeletons cannot expand, so creatures such as the crab must shed their old shell before they can make a new, larger one.

Borrowing a skeleton

1 The hermit crab does not have an exoskeleton of its own and has to find an abandoned shell.

2 When the hermit crab grows bigger, it crawls out of its old shell.

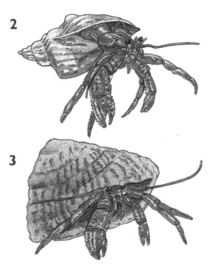

2

1

3

3 The hermit crab finds a larger shell to move into and so its soft body is protected.

Poisonous exoskeleton
The sea urchin has a hard, ball-shaped exoskeleton covered in sharp, poisonous spines. These spines may stick and break off into any animal which touches the sea urchin. This does not hurt the sea urchin.

ARMOUR FOR PROTECTION

Exoskeletons do the same job as bony skeletons, giving animals shape, support and protection. Some exoskeletons have flexible joints, like hinges in armour, that allow the animal to move.

Protecting a delicate body
The giant clam has a huge shell made up of two halves that fit together perfectly when they close.

Large-clawed lobster
A lobster's pincers are strong enough to crush your finger.

Conch shell
Shells grow by adding extra spirals to the original shell.

HEADS AND SKULLS

A skull is a bony case which protects the brain. A baby's skull is very soft. This allows the skull to change shape and helps the baby to squeeze out of the mother's body at birth.

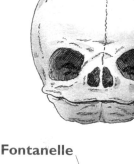

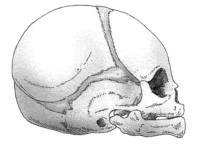

Fontanelle

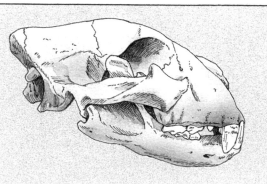

Top of a baby's skull
There is a soft central part of a baby's skull, called the fontanelle. It is usually filled with bone by the time the baby is one year old.

LION'S SKULL
A lion has a large skull with strong jaws and big teeth for catching prey. The muscles which work the jaws are attached to the skull.

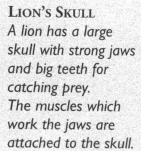

Why we don't all look the same

Although everyone has a similar basic skeleton, the shape of your skull is unique. It directly affects the appearance of your face. Experts can now reconstruct the faces of dead people from their skulls. This has shown how ancient Egyptian Pharaohs might once have looked.

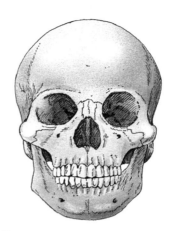

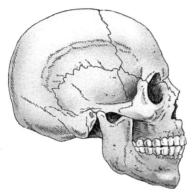

Suture

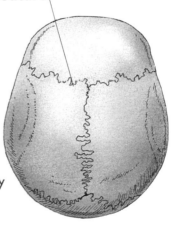

A hole for your nose

There is a hole in the skull where your nose should be. You can bend your nose because it is made of gristly **cartilage**, not bone.

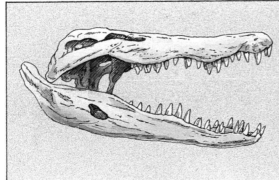

CROCODILE'S SKULL
A crocodile's eyes are set high on the head and its nostrils at the tip of the snout. This helps a crocodile see and breathe while submerged in water.

BACKBONES

Running down the middle of your back is a long chain of bones called your spine or backbone. It is made up of twenty-six **vertebrae**, linked together so that you can twist and bend. The bones also help to protect the **spinal cord**, a delicate bundle of nerves that runs between your brain and body.

Your vertebrae
Your vertebrae are separate bones. You can feel each bone as a knobbly bump along your back. Imagine how difficult life would be if your back was a solid rod of inflexible bone!

Supporting your head
The top two vertebrae, called the atlas and axis, support your skull. The atlas allows you to nod your head up and down, and the axis enables you to shake your head from side-to-side.

Atlas

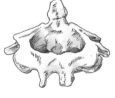

Axis

A tail bone
The lowest four bones of the spine are fused together. In some animals there may be more of these bones, forming a tail.

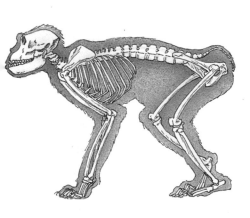

Using four legs
A monkey's skeleton looks similar to a human one, but the spine and **pelvis** are not strong enough to allow the monkey to walk upright on two legs. Monkeys can sometimes stand up on their hind legs, just to look around.

The giraffe
Despite being the tallest animal in the world, a giraffe's neck has the same number of bones as our neck has. Both have seven altogether.

A snake's skeleton
A snake has a very small skull and a long spine, with as many as 400 vertebrae.

PROTECTING YOUR HEART

Your ribs branch off the upper part of your spine and curve round to form a strong cage around the chest. This helps to protect your heart and lungs. The rib cage is flexible and can move up and down to let you breathe in and out.

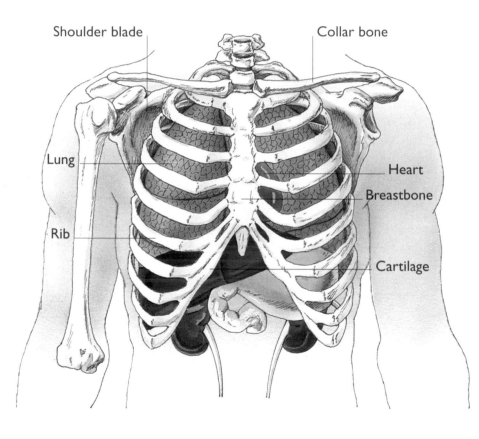

Shoulder blade

Collar bone

Lung

Heart

Breastbone

Rib

Cartilage

Your rib cage

Most people have twelve pairs of ribs. Very few people have eleven or thirteen pairs. The two bottom pairs of ribs, called **floating ribs**, are not attached to the breastbone.

HANDS AND FEET

The digits on our hands and feet are formed from fourteen bones. Fingers and toes are each made up of three bones, apart from our big toes, which are supported by two bones. Thumbs also have two bones in them. The way we move our hands and feet is controlled by muscles and joints.

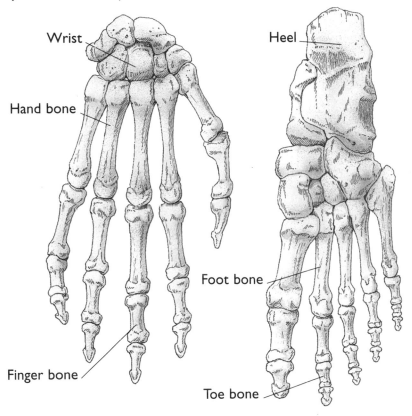

Wrist

Hand bone

Finger bone

Heel

Foot bone

Toe bone

The hand
The five hand bones attach to the eight wrist bones. These form the wrist and allow us to rotate our hands.

The foot
Our toe bones are wider and flatter than those in the fingers. These help to support the weight of our bodies.

A HUMAN SKELETON

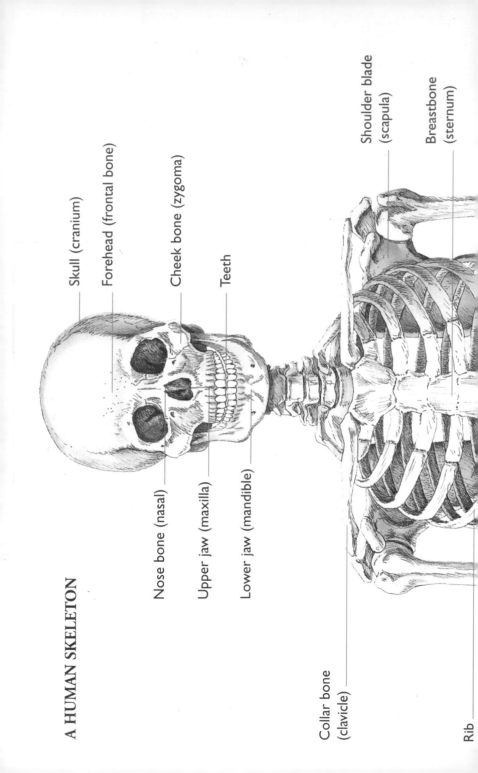

Skull (cranium)

Forehead (frontal bone)

Cheek bone (zygoma)

Teeth

Nose bone (nasal)

Upper jaw (maxilla)

Lower jaw (mandible)

Collar bone (clavicle)

Rib

Shoulder blade (scapula)

Breastbone (sternum)

MOVING PARTS

Your skeleton helps you to move. There are **skeletal muscles** all over your body. Many are attached to bones. Muscles pull on the bones to move different parts of your body, such as your arms and legs. Bones and muscles work together and allow you to run, jump, pick things up and even breathe. Joints are places where two bones meet. They allow you to bend, turn or twist. There are joints all over your body – in your knees, ankles, elbows, shoulders, neck, back and even in your head.

JOINTS AND HOW THEY WORK

HINGE JOINTS
The elbow and knee joints work like hinges. They allow movement back and forth.

SLIDING JOINTS
Between the bones in your back are sliding joints. These enable each vertebra to rotate and slide over one another.

BALL AND SOCKET JOINTS
The shoulder and hip joints work like a ball bearing. This allows movement in several different directions.

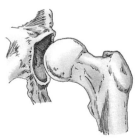

ARMS, LEGS, HANDS AND FEET

Over half the bones in your body are in your arms and hands, legs and feet. They are specially designed to do a variety of jobs. Your arms and hands are built for precision and your legs and feet are built for balance, strength and movement.

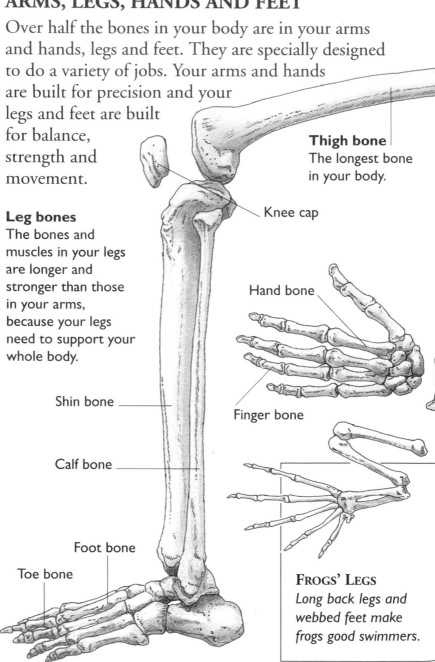

Thigh bone
The longest bone in your body.

Knee cap

Leg bones
The bones and muscles in your legs are longer and stronger than those in your arms, because your legs need to support your whole body.

Hand bone

Shin bone

Finger bone

Calf bone

Foot bone

Toe bone

FROGS' LEGS
Long back legs and webbed feet make frogs good swimmers.

Shoulder blade

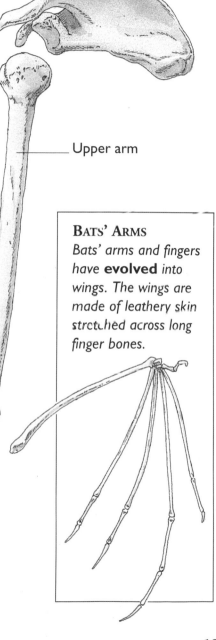

Upper arm

Dexterity
Your hands and arms allow you to perform a range of complex tasks – from picking up tiny pins or playing a musical instrument, to throwing heavy stones.

Lesser forearm bone

Main forearm bone

BATS' ARMS
*Bats' arms and fingers have **evolved** into wings. The wings are made of leathery skin stretched across long finger bones.*

The human thumb
Our thumb only has two finger bones or **phalanges**, whereas the rest of our fingers have three bones. The thumb is very important for grasping objects. Try taping your thumb to your first three fingers. Then, see how difficult it is to write or pick things up.

BIRDS' BONES

Birds' bodies are streamlined and lightweight, especially for flying. Most birds have light, hollow bones. The bones are light because they have lots of air spaces and are strong because they are strengthened by an internal intricate honeycomb frame of stiff, supporting struts.

A falcon's skeleton

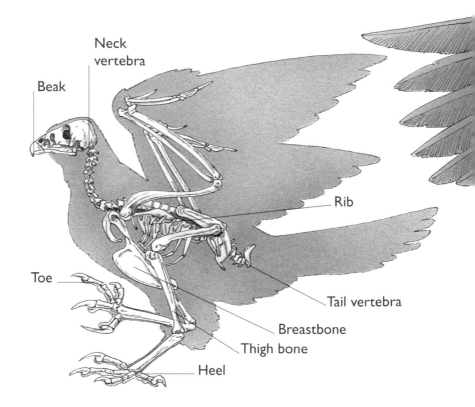

Neck vertebra

Beak

Rib

Toe

Tail vertebra

Breastbone

Thigh bone

Heel

Skulls, teeth and toes

Birds have light skulls with no teeth in their mouths. A bird uses its beak to pick up food.

Most birds have four toes on each foot. One or two toes point backwards to help birds grip.

Birds' front limbs have developed into wings. All birds have wings, but some do not use their wings for flying. Penguins, for example, use their wings as flippers, so they can swim fast underwater. Ostriches use their wings to help them run faster.

A falcon's wing

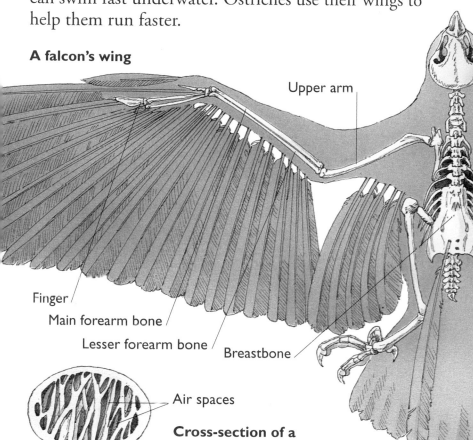

Upper arm

Finger

Main forearm bone

Lesser forearm bone

Breastbone

Air spaces

Cross-section of a bird's bone

Flying

Birds' bones consist of bone tissue and large air spaces. This honeycombed structure makes the bones strong and light.

Powerful flight muscles are attached to a large breastbone. These muscles enable birds to flap their wings.

SEA CREATURES

Animals that live in the sea, for example fish, have skeletons specially adapted for swimming. Instead of limbs, fish have fins to help them move through the water and control their speed and direction. Mammals such as whales and dolphins, which also spend their whole lives in the sea, have flippers, rather than hands and feet. As a result, whales and dolphins can swim very fast. Seals also have flippers. Seals use their flippers to move on land, too.

A fish's skeleton
Muscles attached to the fish's spine produce a side-to-side movement as the fish swims through water.

Fins
Fins are different for each kind of fish. Flatfish, such as plaice, swim using fins which run around the side of the fish's body.

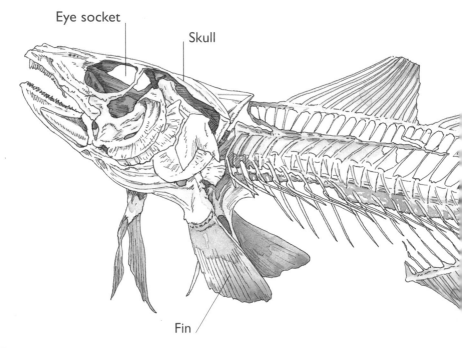

Eye socket

Skull

Fin

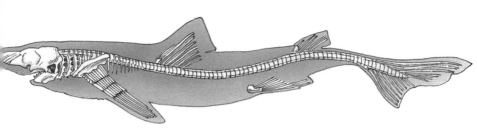

A shark's skeleton

A shark has no bones at all. Its skeleton is made of cartilage. Calcium is present in a shark's backbone, just as it is in ours. A shark's skeleton feels flexible, like our ears.

A turtle's two skeletons

A turtle has a bony skeleton inside its body as well as a hard shell, or exoskeleton, on the outside. It can pull its head and flippers inside its shell, for protection.

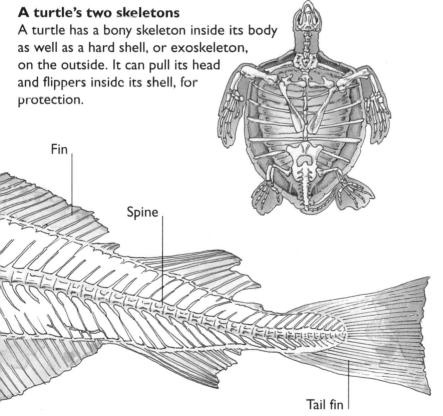

Fin

Spine

Tail fin

BODIES WITHOUT BONES

Some animals have neither a bony skeleton inside their body nor an exoskeleton around them. However, these animals, called invertebrates, have other ways of protecting and looking after themselves.

1 Starfish

A starfish moves along the seabed using tiny tubed feet with suckers at the ends. It feeds on shellfish, prising the shells open with its 'arms'.

2 Earthworm

An earthworm moves through the soil by bunching up and stretching out its body. Slime helps it move and rows of bristly hairs on its body help it to grip.

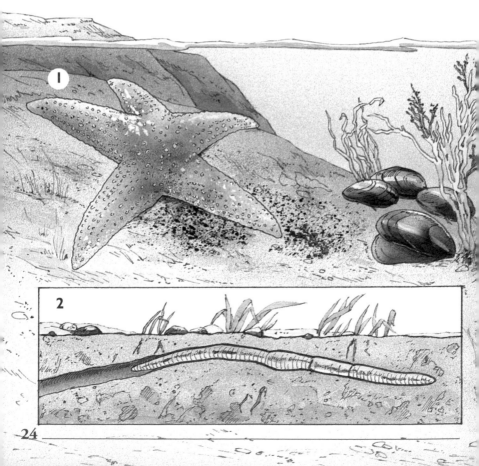

3 Jellyfish

A jellyfish moves through the sea by pumping water in and out of its body. Long tentacles, trailing underneath, are covered in tiny stinging cells and are poisonous enough to harm small fish.

4 Sea fan

A sea fan may look like a plant but it is in fact an animal. Sea fans are covered in thousands of minute tubes that they use to trap food as it moves past in the water.

5 Spanish dancer sea slug

The sea slug protects itself by producing a horrible-tasting substance from its skin. Its bright colour acts as a warning.

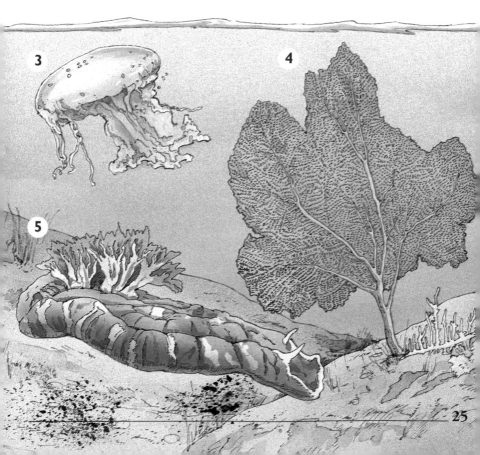

FOSSILS

Bones and shells are hard and long lasting. They remain intact in the ground for millions of years and are gradually turned into stone, and preserved as **fossils**. Most of what we know about **prehistoric** animals, like dinosaurs and early humans, comes from fossil evidence.

Formation of a fossil

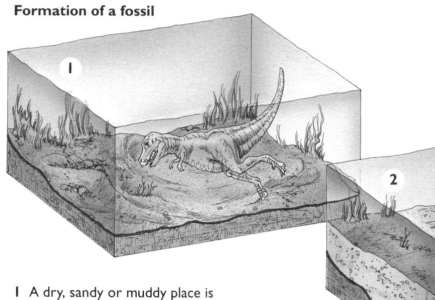

1 A dry, sandy or muddy place is ideal for the formation of fossils. When an animal dies, its soft parts rot away, leaving only the bones. This is why it is rare to find signs of skin on fossils, but in desert areas, the body may simply dry out, leaving the skin. Traces of fossilized dinosaur skin have been found in the Gobi desert in China.
2 Sand or mud builds up over the remains of an animal that has died and over millions of years the remains of the body are slowly transformed into rock. Eggs may also be turned into fossils. From these, we know that some dinosaurs laid eggs, rather than giving birth to live babies.
3 A fossil shows the size and shape of an animal and can also reveal skin markings.

Fossil hunting

Fossils can be deeply embedded in rock. Fossil hunters, or **palaeontologists**, carefully chip away at rocks around a bone, using implements like small hammers and saws. It can take years to piece together a whole dinosaur from the jigsaw of fossil bones.

AMAZING SKELETON FACTS

• **Our bones** The body of a human baby is made up of about 300 bones. Some of these gradually join together, so that the skeleton of an adult consists of 206 bones.

• **Hands and feet** Half of our bones are in our arms, hands, legs and feet.

• **Strength** Bone has the same strength as a hardwood timber such as mahogany.

• **Animal bones** In Asia, the ground down bones of tigers, bears and other large animals are believed to have medicinal powers. Already the tiger is on the edge of extinction, having been illegally hunted for its skeleton.

• **Protection** Seahorses cannot swim fast because their body is encased in bony plates. Their body armour deters other animals from attacking them.

• **Blue whales** Blue whales have the largest skeleton of any animal. They can grow to a length of 35 metres, which is longer than an average swimming pool.

• **Horns and tusks** Both rhinoceros horns and elephant tusks are strong, and resemble bone. But in fact, elephant tusks are modified teeth, and rhino horn is made up of keratin – the same substance that makes our fingernails strong.

• **Giraffe** The world's tallest giraffe measured nearly six metres, taller than a double-decker bus.

GLOSSARY

Cartilage A firm, but flexible substance that may turn into bone.

Evolve To develop naturally over the years.

Exoskeleton A skeleton or shell outside an animal's body.

Floating ribs The bottom two pairs of ribs that are not attached to the breastbone.

Fontanelle The soft part on the top of a baby's skull.

Fossil The remains of a plant or animal that have been turned slowly into rock.

Fracture A break or splinter that occurs when a bone is broken.

Invertebrate An animal without a backbone.

Ligament A fibrous cord which binds bones and joints, and holds organs in place.

Marrow A substance found in spongy bone that makes red blood cells.

Palaeontologist A scientist who uses fossils to learn about previous forms of life.

Pelvis The large bone formation at the base of the spine that supports the back legs of humans and animals.

Phalange A bone in our toes and fingers, and also in the equivalent limbs of other vertebrates.

Prehistoric Something that lived or happened many years ago, before people began writing about events.

Red blood cell A microscopic cell that carries oxygen to parts of the body.

Skeletal muscle A fleshy part of the body that is made of many cells. When these cells change in shape, the muscle moves. This in turn causes the attached bone to move with the muscle.

Spinal cord A delicate bundle of nerves that runs from the brain to the base of the spine, through the backbone, controlling movements and reactions.

Suture A thin, wavy line on the skull that marks where the bones join together.

Tendon A tough, fibrous cord which connects a muscle to a bone.

Vertebra One of the bones that make up the backbone.

Vertebrate An animal that has a backbone.

INDEX *(Entries in **bold** refer to an illustration)*